Make Your Own POM POM PETS

FUN KITS

TOP THAT! Kids™

Copyright © 2003 Top That! Publishing plc
Top That! Publishing, 27023 McBean Parkway, #408 Valencia, CA 91355
Top That! is a Registered Trademark of Top That! Publishing plc
www.topthatpublishing.com

Getting Started

To help you complete the pom pom pets in this book, you will need scissors and some glue. Everything else is provided in the kit!

There are enough pom poms, goggle eyes, and fuzzy sticks in this pack to make all the projects. If you want to make any more projects, and need more supplies, visit your local craft or hobby store.

At the start of each section, it shows you how many pom poms, fuzzy sticks, and goggle eyes you will need to complete each pet.

Note: Pom pom colors may vary from those pictured.

Safety: Make sure that you ask an adult to help you when using scissors.

Pet Tricks

Here are some of the moves you'll need to master to complete the models in this book.

Glueing Thread
Part the pom pom fabric and apply a small amount of glue. Insert the required length of thread and hold it in place for 30 seconds to help it stick.

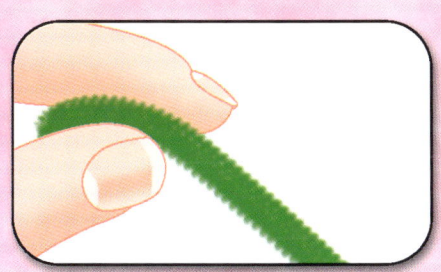

Shaping
Use your thumb and forefinger to bend the fuzzy sticks into the correct shape.

Glueing Pom Poms
Hold glued pom poms together for at least 30 seconds to help them stick.

Milly Mouse

This cute little mouse will make the sweetest of pets.

You will need:
- one gray pom pom (1.2 in.)
- two pink pom poms (0.6 in.)
- one pink fuzzy stick
- a pair of goggle eyes
- 2.4 in. of black thread
- glue

Pom Pom Size Guide

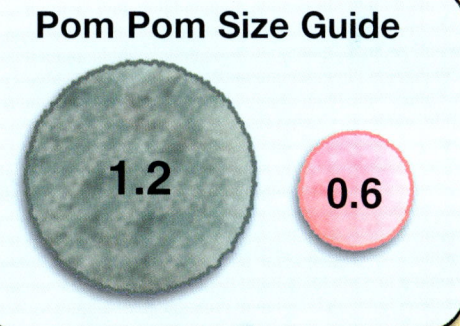

1 Take the large gray pom pom and roll it between the palms of your hands to lengthen it. This will become Milly's body. Rolling will create a larger base area, allowing her to sit well.

2 For Milly's ears, wrap a piece of pink fuzzy stick around the outside of each pink pom pom, and twist to secure. Glue into position on her body, then add the goggle eyes.

3 Cut 2.4 in. of black thread into three equal pieces (0.8 in. each), place them together, and knot in the center. This makes a set of whiskers and a nose. Use a small amount of glue to stick it in place.

4 Use the remainder of the pink fuzzy stick for her tail. To make a wiggly tail, simply bend a few little kinks. Glue one end to the underside of the body for a neat finish.

Chris Caterpillar

Creepy crawlies can be cute too!

You will need:
- four yellow pom poms (1 in.)
- four green pom poms (1 in.)
- one yellow pom pom (0.6 in.)
- one green pom pom (0.6 in.)
- one yellow pom pom (0.4 in.)
- one green pom pom (0.4 in.)
- 2 in. (approx.) black thread
- a pair of goggle eyes
- glue
- scissors

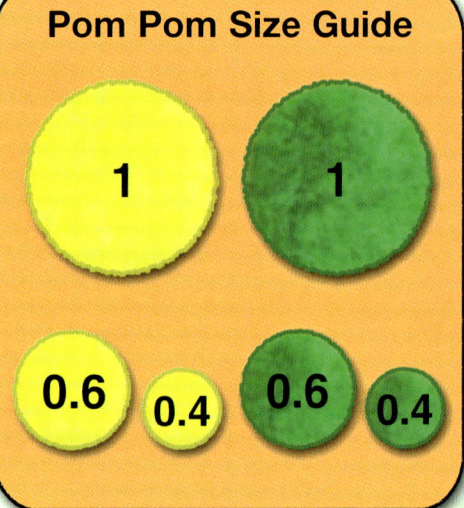

Pom Pom Size Guide

1 Glue the yellow and green pom poms together, alternately, yellow, green, yellow, green, and so on. Start with the larger 1 in. pom poms (head end) and then work down to the 0.4 in. pom poms (tail end). Pay particular attention to Chris's body shape when glueing your pom poms together. Why not create an arch in his back to make it look as if he is crawling along?

Gary Goldfish

A groovy little goldfish that's great fun to make.

You will need:

- one orange pom pom (1.6 in.)
- two orange pom poms (0.4 in.)
- four orange fuzzy sticks
- 0.8 in. of black thread
- a pair of goggle eyes
- glue

Pom Pom Size Guide

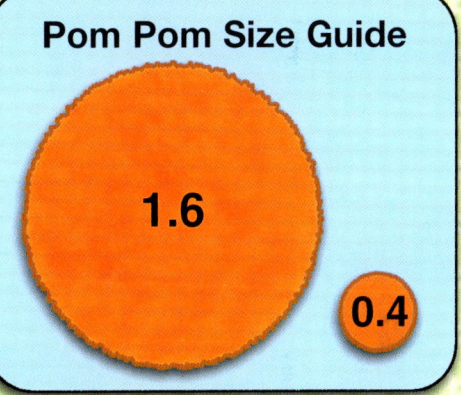

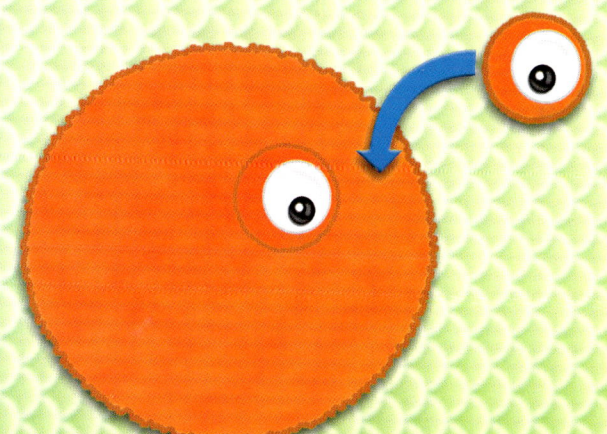

1 Take the large orange pom pom and glue the two smaller pom poms onto it to create Gary's bulging eyes. On the end of each of these, add the goggle eyes.

11

2 To make a beautiful tail fin, take two orange fuzzy sticks and link them together with a twist. The shape of the tail fin is made by winding the fuzzy stick backward and forward upon itself, with shorter segments in the center. Once you are happy with its shape, glue firmly into position onto Gary's body.

3 Using the same technique, take half an orange fuzzy stick to create each side fin and again glue firmly in place.

4 Use the remaining fuzzy stick to create his dorsal fin on the top of his back. Again, use the same technique as before but try to create more of an arch shape.

5 To finish, give Gary a happy smile. Take 0.8 in. of black thread and tie a knot at each end. Dab a small amount of glue on each knot, and carefully position it on his face.

Perky Piglet

This perky little pig will melt your heart!

You will need:

- one pink pom pom (1.4 in.)
- one pink pom pom (1 in.)
- four pink pom poms (0.6 in.)
- one pink fuzzy stick
- a pair of goggle eyes
- glue
- scissors

Pom Pom Size Guide

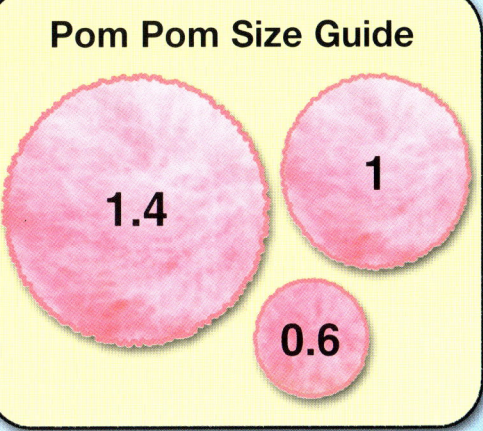

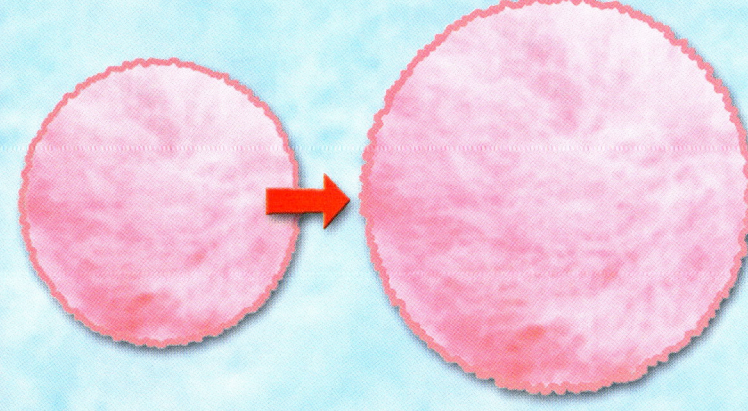

1 Take the medium pom pom (this will become the piglet's head), and glue to one end of the large pom pom (the body).

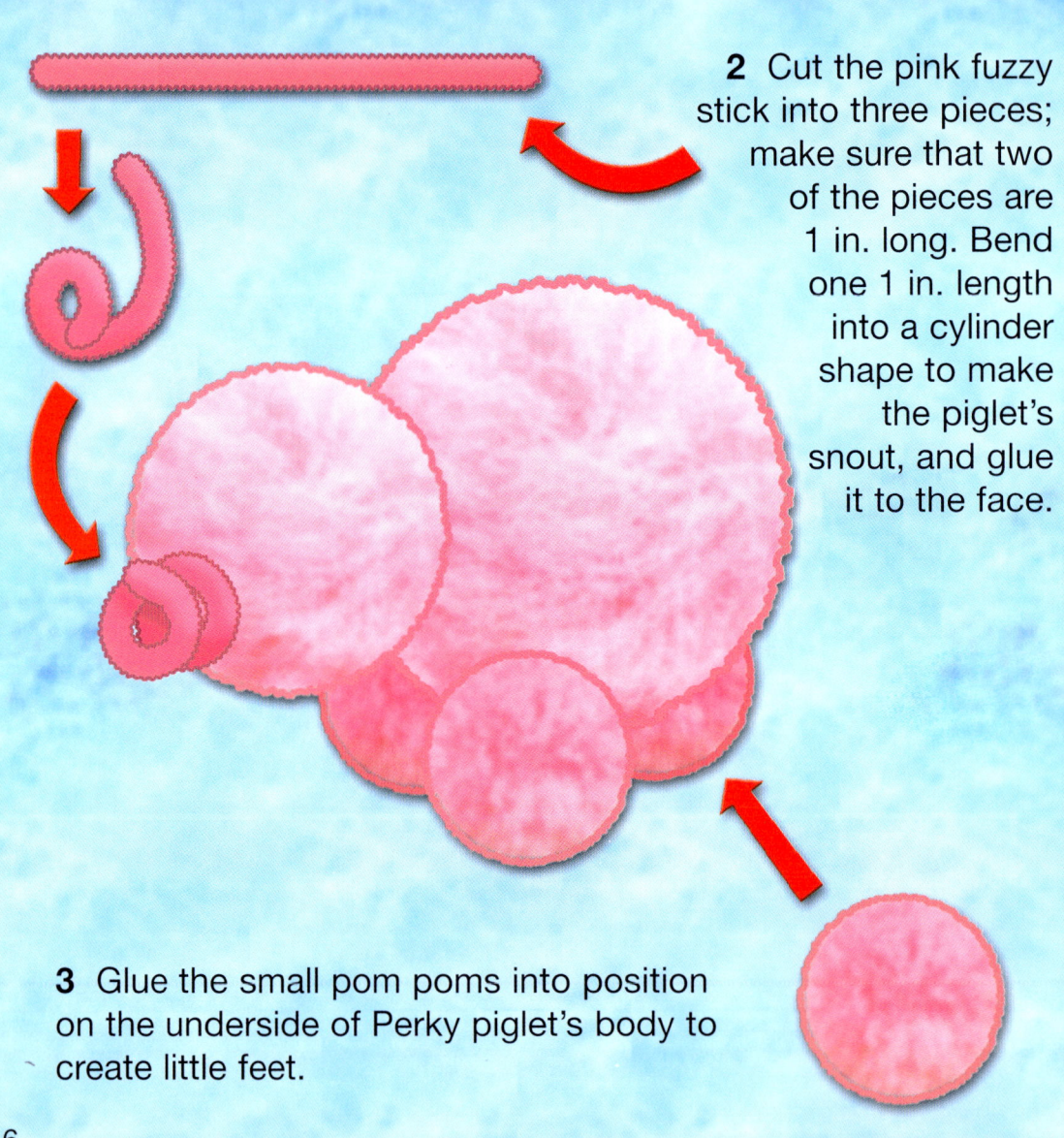

2 Cut the pink fuzzy stick into three pieces; make sure that two of the pieces are 1 in. long. Bend one 1 in. length into a cylinder shape to make the piglet's snout, and glue it to the face.

3 Glue the small pom poms into position on the underside of Perky piglet's body to create little feet.

4 Using the long piece of the pink fuzzy stick, make two triangular-shaped ears. Glue them into position.

5 To create a curly piglet's tail, bend the other 1 in. piece of the pink fuzzy stick into a coil shape. Carefully glue it into position.

6 To finish, add a pair of goggle eyes.

Robbie the Rabbit

It's easy to make Robbie the lovely fluffy bunny!

You will need:
- one light brown pom pom (1.4 in.)
- one light brown pom pom (1 in.)
- one white pom pom (0.6 in.)
- one pink fuzzy stick
- two light brown fuzzy stick
- a small piece of white paper
- a pair of goggle eyes
- glue
- scissors

Pom Pom Size Guide

1 Glue the smaller 1 in. light brown pom pom on top of the larger 1.4 in. pom pom. This is Robbie's head and body.

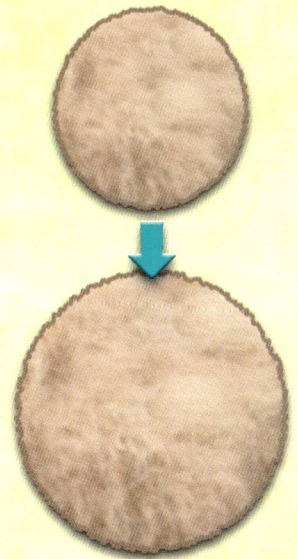

2 For the inner of Robbie's ear, cut the pink fuzzy stick into three pieces; make sure that two pieces are 1.2 in. each. Cut a small piece off one brown fuzzy stick. Cut the large piece of the brown fuzzy stick in half and wrap each piece around the outside of the two 1.2 in. pieces of pink fuzzy stick, securing with a twist. When glueing this to Robbie, add a little character by bending over one ear.

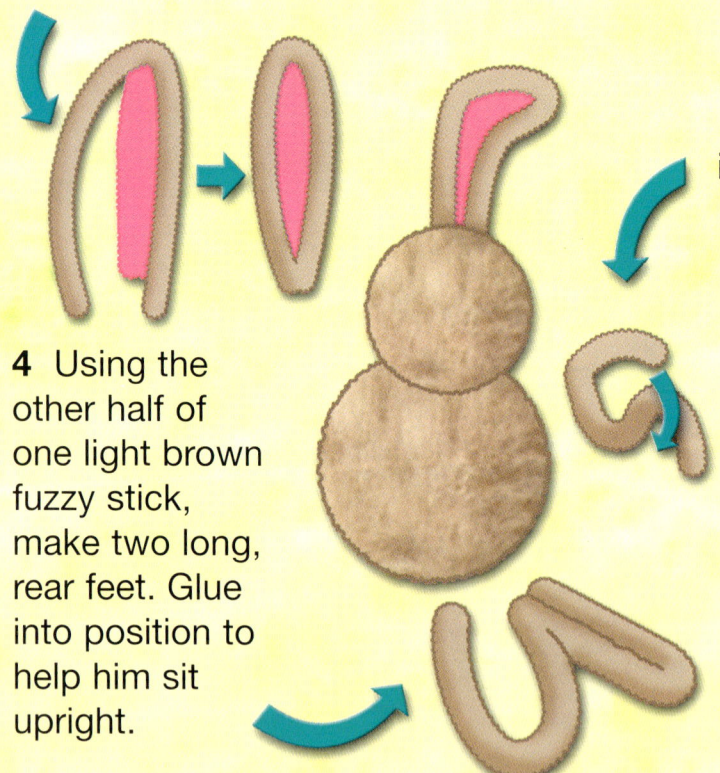

3 Cut the other brown fuzzy stick in half and use one half to make his two front feet. Curve them to look as if he is holding them up. This often occurs when rabbits stand up on their rear legs to take a look around.

4 Using the other half of one light brown fuzzy stick, make two long, rear feet. Glue into position to help him sit upright.

5 Bend the small offcut of the light brown fuzzy stick into a simple figure eight shape. Glue it to Robbie's face to create his cheeks and mouth.

6 A very important characteristic to remember are his front teeth. Cut these from a small piece of white paper and glue in place.

7 For the finishing touches, add a pair of goggle eyes and a small white 0.6 in. pom pom for his tail.

Daisy Duck

Four easy steps is all it takes to make this dainty duck.

You will need:
- one white pom pom (1.6 in.)
- one light gray pom pom (1 in.)
- one green pom pom (1.2 in.)
- one yellow fuzzy stick
- one white fuzzy stick
- two brown fuzzy sticks
- a pair of goggle eyes
- glue

Pom Pom Size Guide

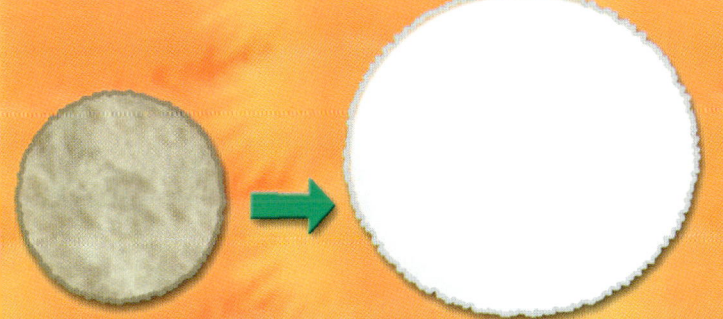

1 Glue the light gray pom pom to the front of the large white pom pom.

2 To create Daisy's head, glue the green pom pom onto the light gray pom pom.

3 Use the yellow fuzzy stick to make her beak. Simply wrap it around on itself to create the shape. Glue it firmly into place.

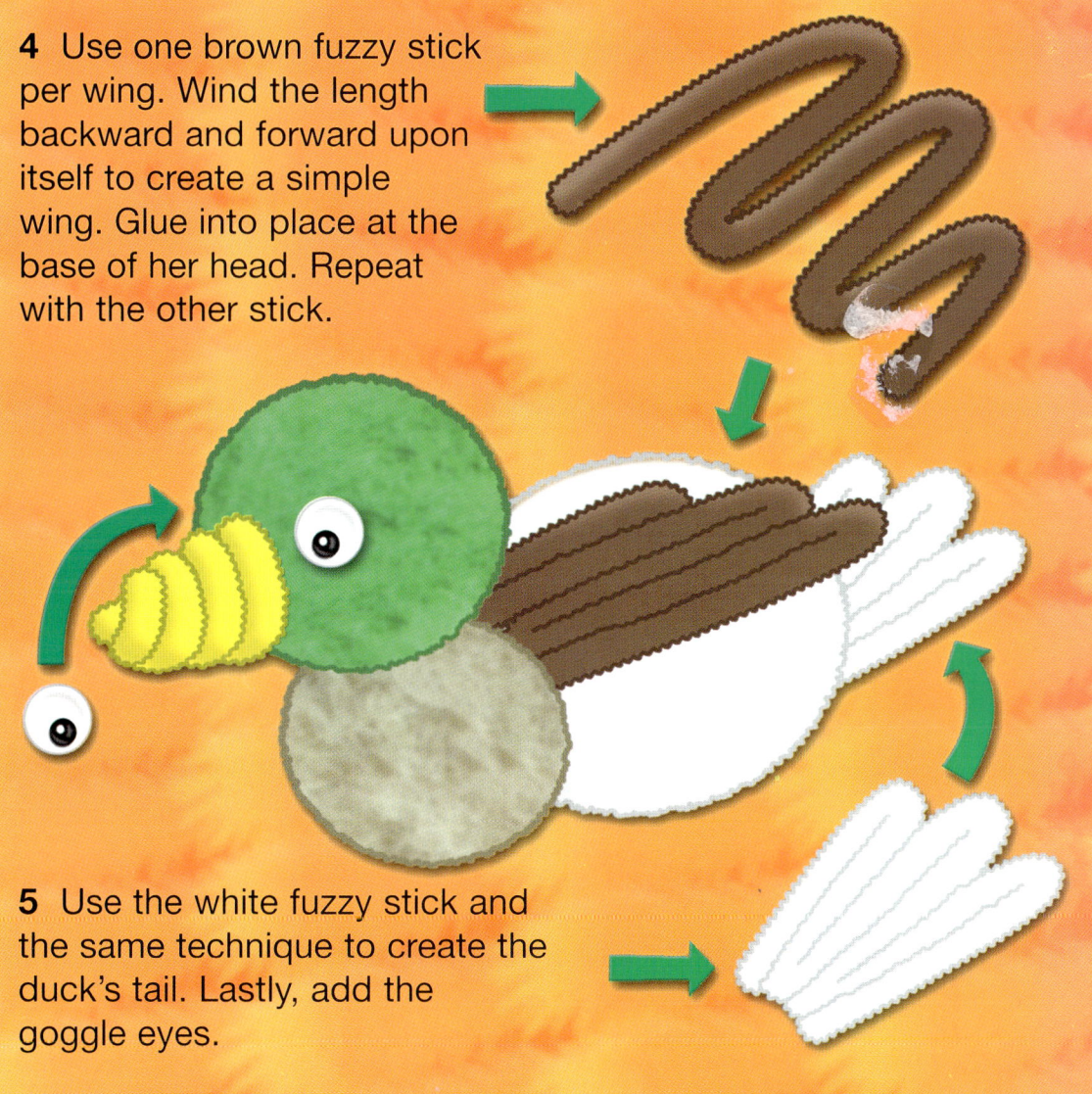

4 Use one brown fuzzy stick per wing. Wind the length backward and forward upon itself to create a simple wing. Glue into place at the base of her head. Repeat with the other stick.

5 Use the white fuzzy stick and the same technique to create the duck's tail. Lastly, add the goggle eyes.

Parisian Poodle

Pom poms make the perfect pooch in no time!

You will need:
- two white pom poms (1.6 in.)
- one white pom pom (1.2 in.)
- four white pom poms (0.8 in.)
- one white pom pom (0.6 in.)
- eight white pom poms (0.4 in.)
- half a red fuzzy stick
- half a yellow fuzzy stick
- a pair of goggle eyes
- glue

Pom Pom Size Guide

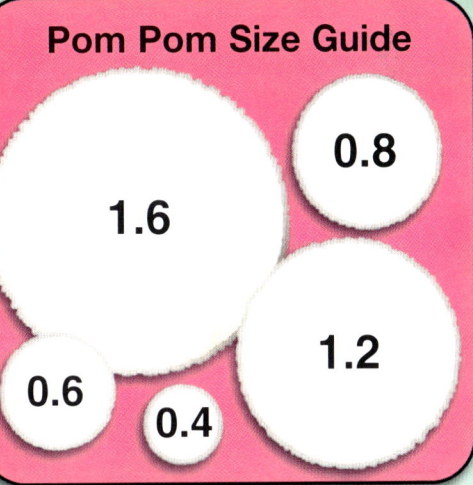

1 Attach the two large 1.6 in. pom poms together, to form the poodle's body. Glue the 1.2 in. pom pom to one end of the body, to form the poodle's head.

2 Poodles are well known for their distinctive pom pom-style haircuts, and creating a realistic pet is simple. Take half a white fuzzy stick per leg and, at one end, glue a 0.8 in. pom pom for the hip joint. Approximately halfway down the leg, create the knee by glueing one 0.4 in. pom pom and, at the end, add another 0.4 in. pom pom for the paw. Repeat this for all four legs and glue them firmly into position.

3 You will need a small piece of white fuzzy stick (0.8 in.) for your poodle's tail. Glue a 0.6 in. pom pom on the head. Attach to your poodle in a fairly upright position.

4 To make your poodle's large floppy ears, take a white fuzzy stick and use half to make a triangular shape. Wrap the excess around the structure to cover it completely. The muzzle of your poodle is created by simply coiling up a short length of white fuzzy stick into a cone shape. Gently glue into position.

5 For a finishing touch to your poodle, add a collar and ID tag around its neck. To create this, simply wrap a short length of red fuzzy stick around the poodle's neck for the collar and then coil a small piece of yellow fuzzy stick into a circle for the ID tag. Then glue firmly in place on the front of the collar. To finish, add the goggle eyes.

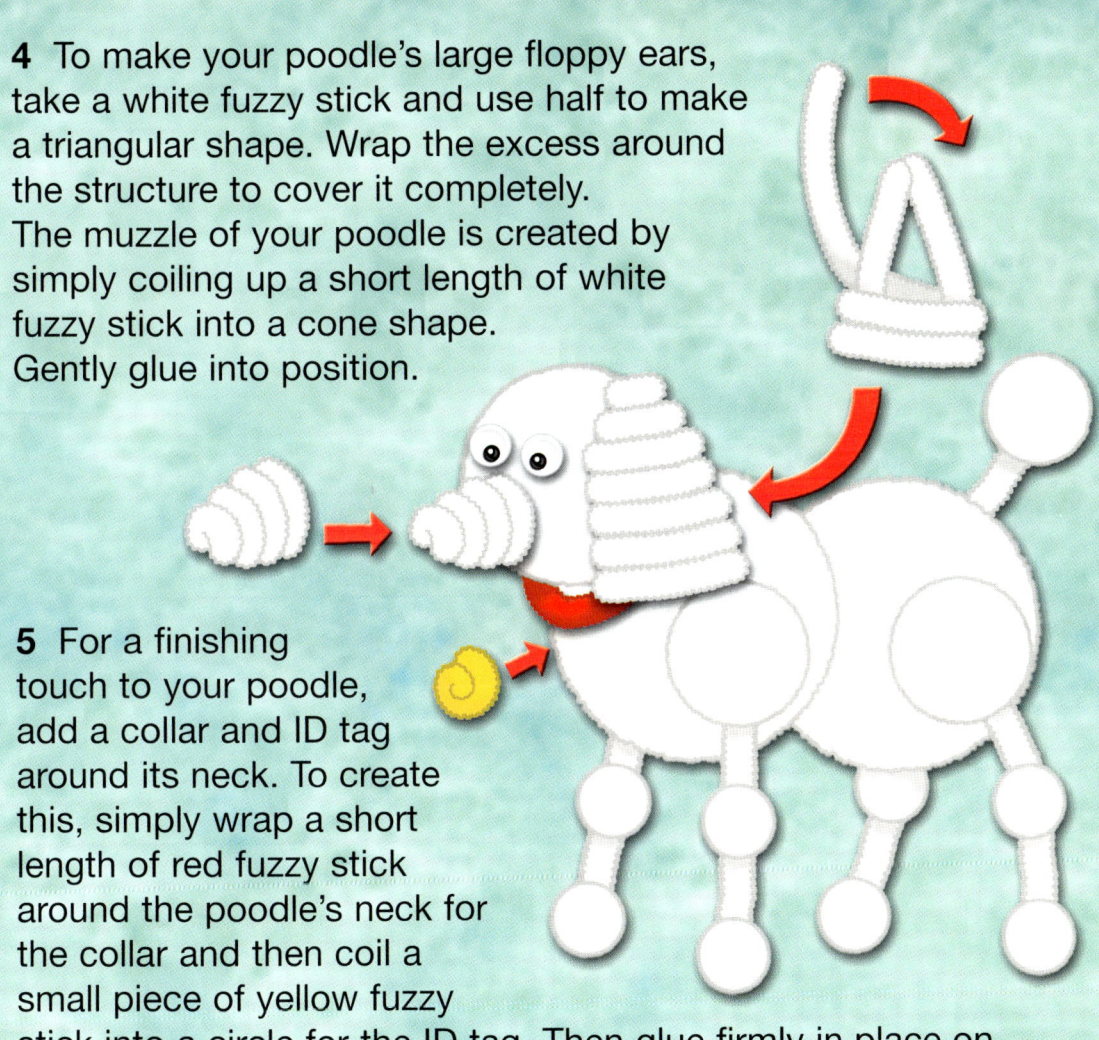

Polly Parrot

A simple-to-make feathered friend.

You will need:
- one green pom pom (1.4 in.)
- two green pom poms (1 in.)
- three green fuzzy sticks
- three brown fuzzy sticks
- half a red fuzzy stick
- half a yellow fuzzy stick
- half a gray fuzzy stick
- a pair of goggle eyes
- glue

Pom Pom Size Guide

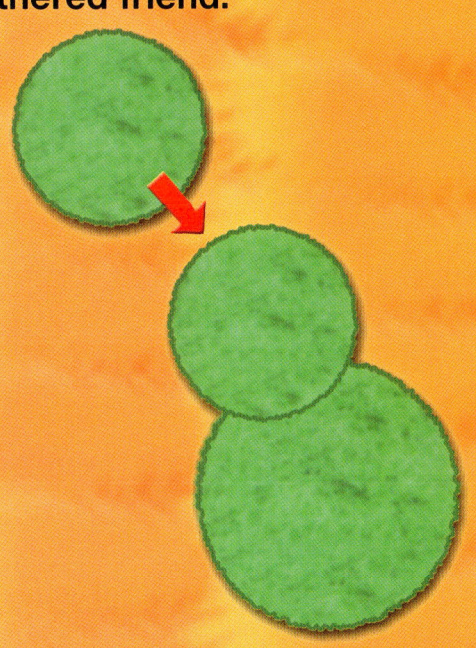

1 Glue the head and body pom poms together, the larger 1.4 in. pom pom should be on the bottom and the two 1 in. poms stacked on top.

2 To create Polly's wings, you will need one green fuzzy stick per wing. Bend the fuzzy stick backward and forward on itself, creating a simple fan shape. Repeat this for the other wing, then glue firmly in place on either side.

3 Her tail is created in much the same way as the wings, by folding the fuzzy stick backward and forward. You will need one fuzzy stick to create a reasonably sized tail. Glue firmly to the underside of the body for a neat finish.

4 Bend a small offcut of red fuzzy stick into a curved shape and glue into position. On top of this, glue two circles made from a small piece of coiled yellow fuzzy stick. These circles create an ideal base for her goggle eyes, helping them to really stand out.

5 Polly's beak is made from approximately half a gray fuzzy stick. Decide how long you want the beak to be, then wrap the excess around one end. Glue it into place.

6 Finally, cut six equal lengths of brown fuzzy stick (approx. 0.8 in. each). Twist and lock three of them together at one end. Repeat this with the other three pieces to create a pair of claws. Glue firmly to the underside of the body for a neat finish.

7 To make a simple perch for Polly, use the remaining two brown fuzzy sticks to construct an arch. Attach her feet to the arch so that she stands steady.

Carrie the Cat

A purr-fect pet that's easy to make.

You will need:
- two black pom poms (1.2 in.)
- two black pom poms (1 in.)
- one black pom pom (0.8 in.)
- two black pom poms (0.4 in.)
- three black fuzzy sticks
- half a white fuzzy stick
- 2.4 in. black thread
- a pair of goggle eyes
- glue
- scissors

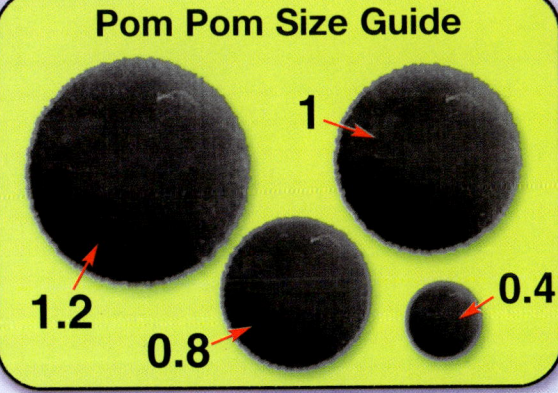

Pom Pom Size Guide

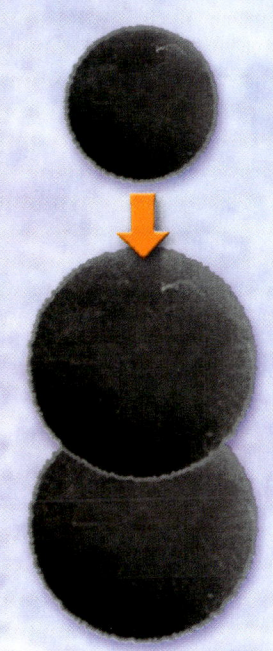

1 Glue the two 1.2 in. pom poms together, and then place a 0.8 in. pom pom on top to form Carrie's head.

2 To create her hips and make it look as if she is sitting down, glue the two 1 in. pom poms either side of the lower 1.2 in. pom pom.

3 To make her legs, you will need approximately half a black fuzzy stick per leg. At the end of each leg, double up the thickness by winding the fuzzy stick back on itself, to create the paws. Why not add a small piece of white fuzzy stick around one paw?

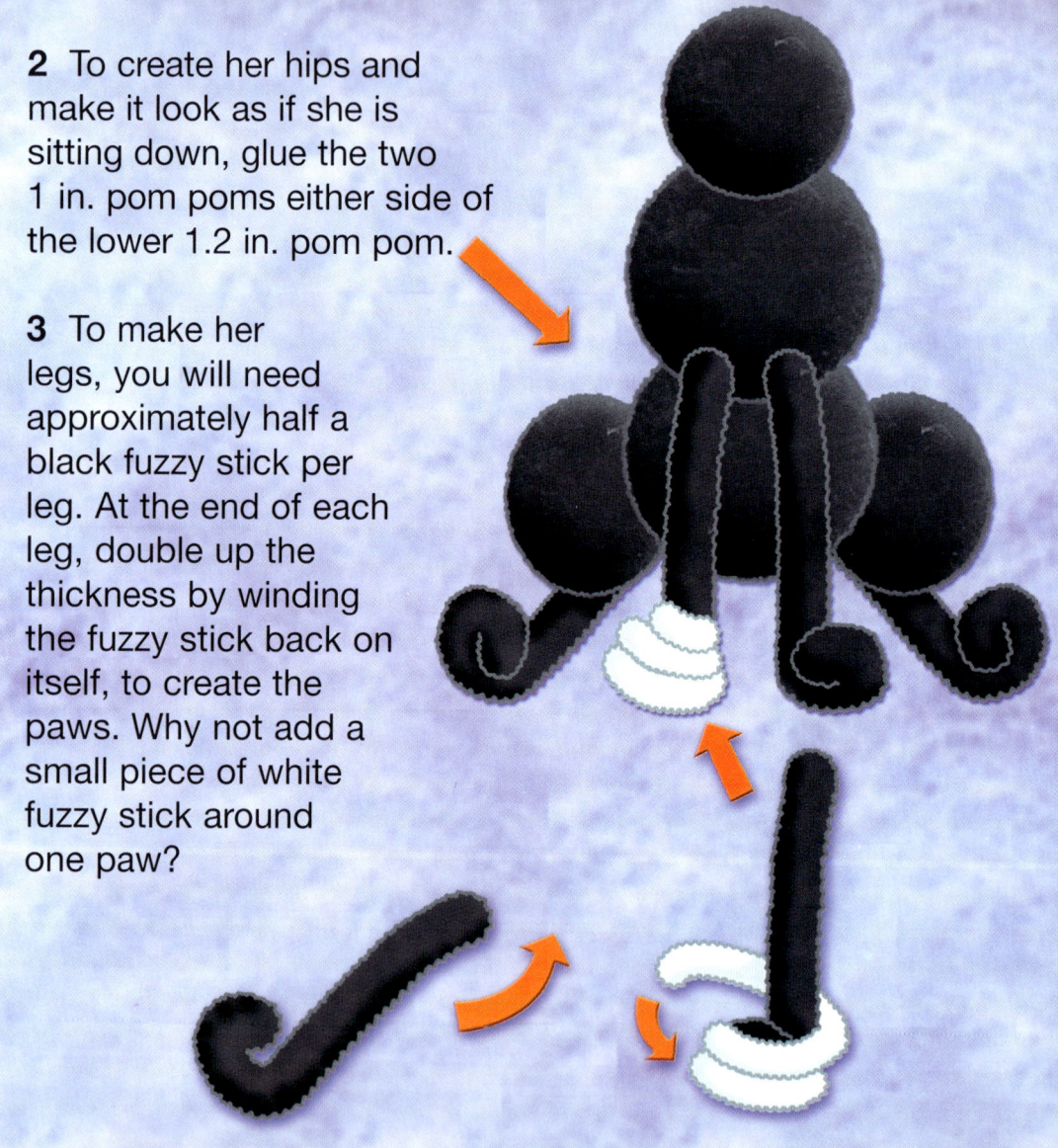

4 To make a realistic face, glue on the two 0.4 in. pom poms side by side to create a perfect pair of cheeks and a mouth. On top of the head, glue two triangular-shaped ears, made from approximately 0.8 in. of black fuzzy stick per ear.

5 Her nose and whiskers are created from three lengths of black thread (0.8 in.). These are simply knotted together in the center and, glued into position. Add the goggle eyes.

6 To finish, use the remaining black fuzzy stick to create a tail for Carrie. Finish with a little offcut of white fuzzy stick on the tip of the tail.

Red, Red Robin

A chirpy little creature!

You will need:
- one white pom pom (1.6 in.)
- two red pom poms (1 in.)
- four brown fuzzy sticks
- one red fuzzy stick
- one gray fuzzy stick
- half a light brown fuzzy stick
- a pair of goggle eyes
- glue
- scissors

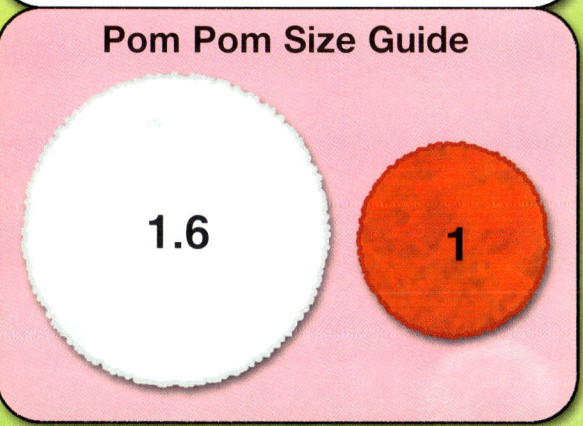

Pom Pom Size Guide

1.6   1

1 Glue the two red 1 in. pom poms together and then glue them firmly on top of the large white pom pom, slightly off-center.

2 Next, take two brown fuzzy sticks and fold them in half. Glue the folded ends to the top of the robin's head as well as securing the rest of the length down the robin's back. Twist together any extra length that stretches further than the robin's body, then fan out to create a tail.

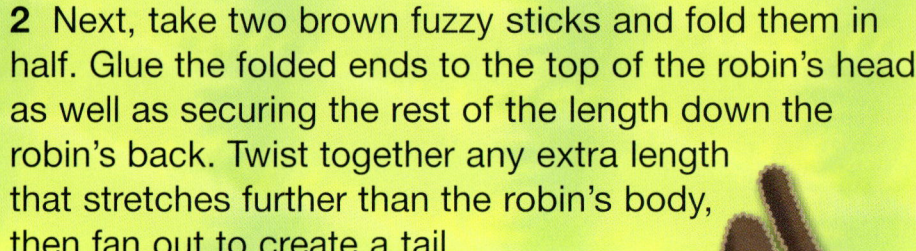

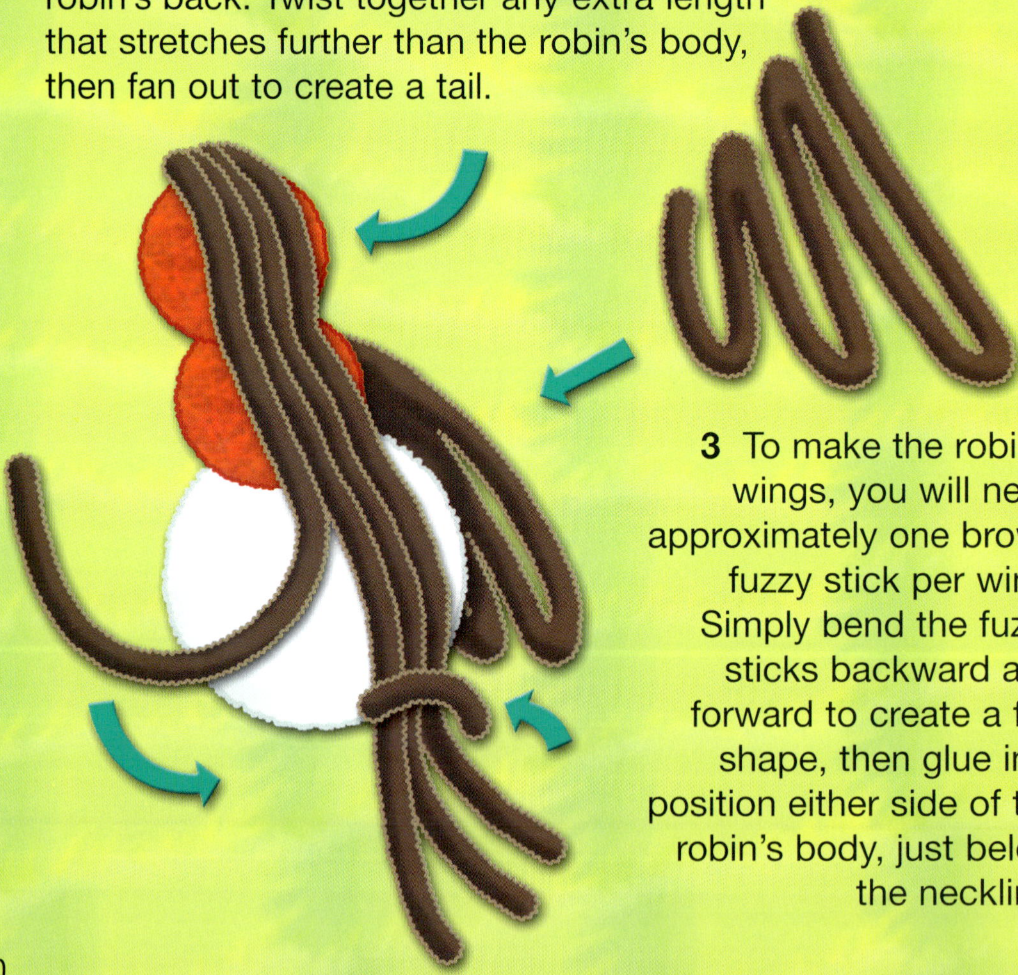

3 To make the robin's wings, you will need approximately one brown fuzzy stick per wing. Simply bend the fuzzy sticks backward and forward to create a fan shape, then glue into position either side of the robin's body, just below the neckline.

4 To finish, use the short length of light brown fuzzy stick to make the beak. Decide how long you want your robin's beak to be and then wrap around the excess at one end. Attach this end to the robin's face, followed by the goggle eyes.

5 To create feet, cut the gray fuzzy stick into six equal lengths. Take three lengths and twist together at one end, leaving the other end open, to create three claws. Repeat this for the other leg, then glue both to the underside of the robin. Finally, cut the red fuzzy stick into two pieces, each 1.2 in. long. Fold these in half and then stick onto the robin's chest.

Carmen the Chameleon

Make this exotic creature to brighten up your pet collection.

You will need:
- two light green pom poms (1 in.)
- two light green pom poms (0.8 in.)
- five light green fuzzy sticks
- a pair of goggle eyes
- glue

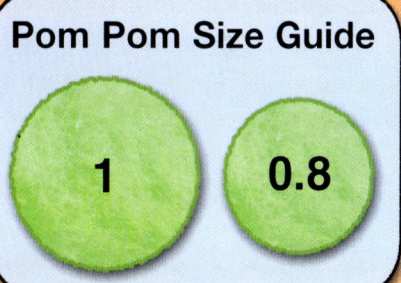

Pom Pom Size Guide

1 Glue the three pom poms together in a row, remembering that the slightly larger pom pom is Carmen's head.

2 Creating her arched back is simple. Bend a length of one fuzzy stick into an arch shape, to create a structure. Now wrap the excess of the fuzzy stick around the structure until you can no longer see a gap between the top of the arch and the original back, then glue firmly into place, on the pom poms.

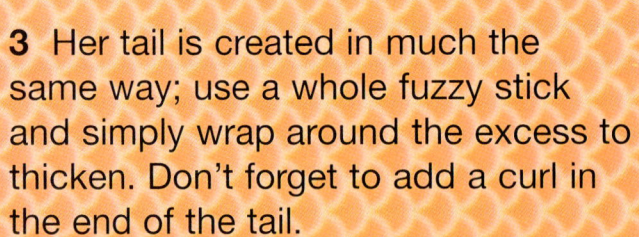

3 Her tail is created in much the same way; use a whole fuzzy stick and simply wrap around the excess to thicken. Don't forget to add a curl in the end of the tail.

4 Chameleons have huge bulging eye sockets. Cut half a fuzzy stick in two and coil up each length into cone shapes. Glue these into position on either side of her head. On the end of each of these eye sockets, attach the goggle eyes. Use the remainder of the halved fuzzy stick to create a small fan shape to be glued in place for her collar.

5 Use the last two green fuzzy sticks to make the legs. Use approximately half a fuzzy stick per leg. Bend at the end of each leg to create two toes so she can grip onto various objects.

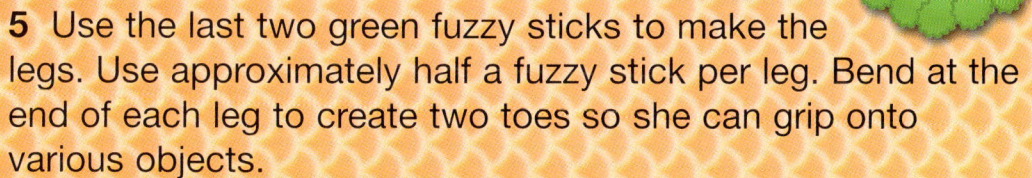

Hattie Hamster

You only need three pom poms to create Hattie.

You will need:
- one brown and white mix pom pom (1.6 in.)
- two light brown pom poms (0.6 in.)
- half a brown fuzzy stick
- 2.4 in. of black thread
- a pair of goggle eyes
- glue
- scissors

Pom Pom Size Guide

1 First, cut a 0.4 in. length of brown fuzzy stick, then cut the remainder in half. Wrap the two lengths of fuzzy stick around the outside of the two light brown pom poms, securing with a twist. Glue firmly to the large brown and white 1.6 in. pom pom (the body).

2 Next cut three equal lengths of black thread (0.8 in.) to create Hattie's nose and whiskers. Simply knot together in the center and then carefully glue onto her face. Then add a pair of goggle eyes.

3 Finally, add Hattie's tiny tail, made from the 0.4 in. offcut of the brown fuzzy stick.